The Iltis in the country.

VW Iltis

von Willy Queißner

The goal in the development of the Iltis was to create a stock off-road vehicle with passenger-car qualities and optimal mobility on and off the road, as well as outstanding economy thanks to a low weight.

The military requirements formed an essential basis for this vehicle's performance description. In this book the conception of the vehicle will be portrayed, with the running-gear design and the arrangement of aggregates deliberately downplayed. Using the engine and gearbox as an example, it will be shown how suitable engines could be created for such a high-performance vehicle on the basis of existing passenger-car components which were expanded on and modified. Many photos and drawings complete this report. Particular emphasis has been placed on offering large-scale pictures, so the reader will be able to recognize the smallest details.

The Concept

The development of the stock VW off-road vehicle, begun in the autumn of 1975, was based on German military requirements. The following had been stated in print:

- The main dimensions of the vehicle and the number of seats;
- An effective load limit of 500 kilograms over and above the basic military equipment.

Schiffer Military History
Atglen, PA

Rear view of a test vehicle. The arrangement of the spare wheel and gasoline can are easy to see.

- Ground clearance, tilt angle, and fording depth (60 centimeters);
- A low-gear speed of at most 4 kph on a 50% grade for a vehicle at the load limit;
- The vehicle should be driveable between -30 and +40 degrees;
- Optional four-wheel drive and differential lock;
- The use of as many stock parts as possible;
- The least possible need of maintenance;
- Adherence to the safety requirements of German and international traffic laws.

The Iltis has no divider drive, but rather a suitably modified Audi gearbox, with a switch for off-road and reverse gears added, attached to the engine block. The front-axle drive is integrated into this system. The driveshaft leading to the rear axle is driven by the pinion drive. The front-axle components are almost identical to those of the rear axle. The advantages of this design are obvious, considering the size of the vehicle:
- Only one cardan driveshaft with two joints;
- Few bearing parts that need to be sealed;
- Low weight;
- Low center of gravity;
- No lock needed between the axles;
- Sufficient transmission via appropriate drive separation;
- Sufficient axle load on the front axle from the front-mounted motor.

The Motor

The powerplant of the VW Iltis is an in-line four-cylinder motor, such as has already proved itself well in numerous VW vehicles. The Iltis version, though, has a displacement of 1.7 liters. The bore and stroke are those of the 5-cylinder motor of this series, and thus have the same modern piston-engine characteristics. The power of 55 kW (75 HP) is attained at 5,500 rpm, the maximum torque of 135 Nm (13.5 kpm) at 2,800 rpm. The fuel used is 91 ROZ, this being regular gasoline.

Air is taken in through a dry-air filter with mechanical pre-separation, with air entry always, even in the cold-air phase, taking place at a protected site by the water box. Fuel is supplied by an electric fuel pump, which is housed safely in the rear of the vehicle. Cooling is done by a heavy-metal radiator with side water box and two thermostatically controllable electric fans with flat motors. Depending on the heat, either both fans or just one will be in operation.

The 24-volt electric system follows military requirements and is protected from water and spray for use in action. A masked light and starter box are provided. Two batteries under the rear seats are easy to reach. The halogen headlights have a a high-low beam regulator.

Translated from the German by Ed Force

Printed in China.
ISBN: 0-7643-1309-6

This book was originally published under the title, *Fahrzeug Profile-VW - Iltis* by Flugzeug Publikation, GmbH

We are interested in hearing from authors with book ideas on related topics.

Published by Schiffer Publishing Ltd.
4880 Lower Valley Road
Atglen, PA 19310
Phone: (610) 593-1777
FAX: (610) 593-2002
E-mail: Schifferbk@aol.com.
Visit our web site at: www.schifferbooks.com
Please write for a free catalog.
This book may be purchased from the publisher.
Please include $3.95 postage.
Try your bookstore first.

In Europe, Schiffer books are distributed by:
Bushwood Books
6 Marksbury Ave.
Kew Gardens
Surrey TW9 4JF
England
Phone: 44 (0) 20 8392-8585
FAX: 44 (0) 20 8392-9876
E-mail: Bushwd@aol.com.
Free postage in the UK. Europe: air mail at cost.
Try your bookstore first.

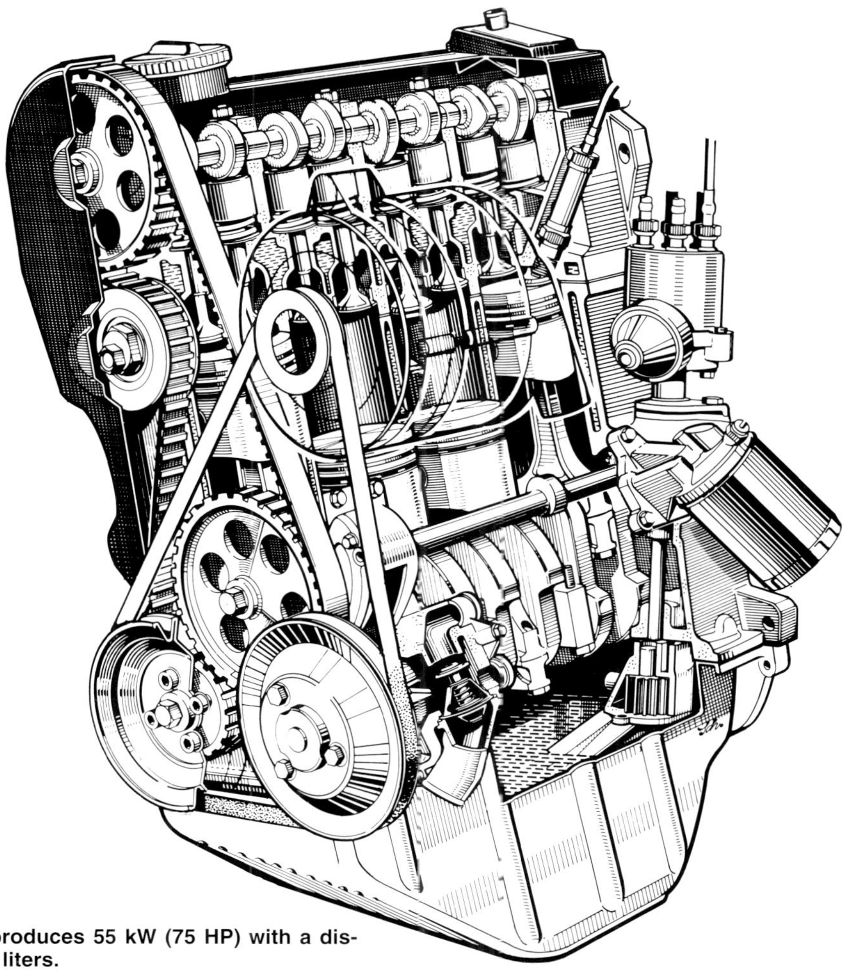

The Iltis motor produces 55 kW (75 HP) with a displacement of 1.7 liters.

Drawing of the pre-production model (without scale).

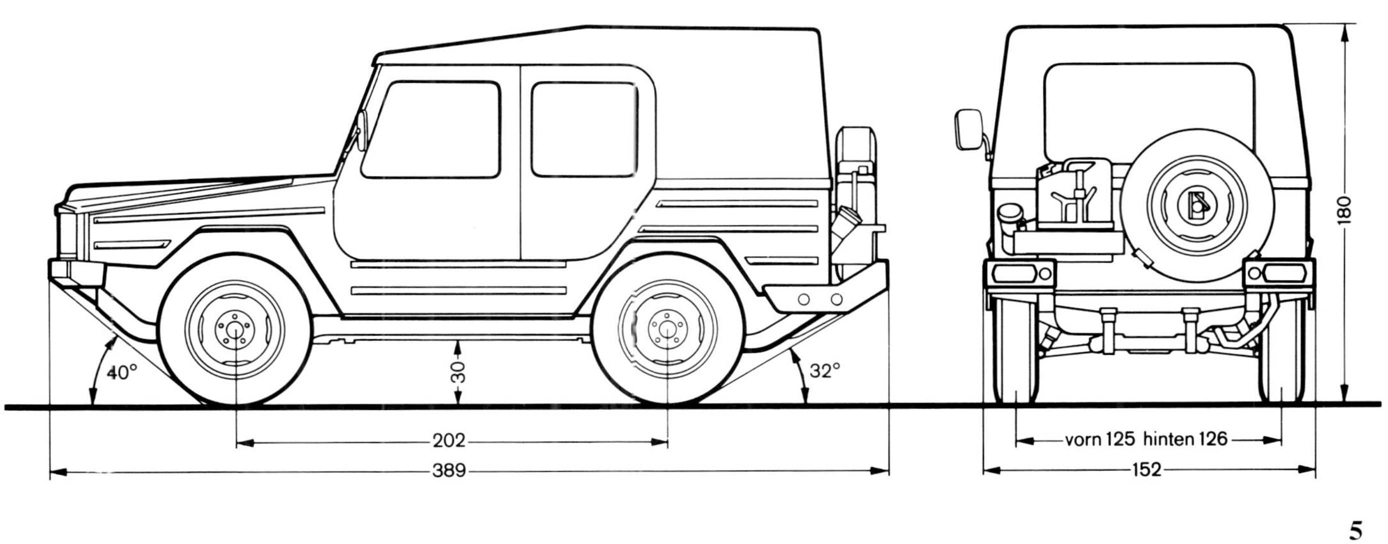

Test vehicle 01 with top up.

Here the top has been folded eas ly.

A good view from the side; at first the top had zippers.

The Gearbox

From the single-plate dry clutch, the torque goes into the combined shifting and dividing gearbox with its integrated front-axle differential. The multipart housing is built low and flanged onto the engine block. When all-wheel drive is switched on, four forward speeds are available, with ratios of 7.3, 3.9, 2.7, 1.4, and 1.0. The 7.3 gear is only needed in practice on steep inclines. With all-wheel drive switched off, there is no equalization between the front and rear axles. When the rear-axle drive is switched on, four forward speeds can be utilized.

For use as an all-terrain vehicle, it is vital that all moving parts of the drive train from the gearbox to both ends of the cardan shaft and at the ends of the shafts to drive the wheels are dependably sealed. These sealings must do their job reliably during hours of use in muddy and damp soils.

The Running Gear

The rear wheel of the running gear is a ladder frame with two longitudinal members in closed box form, heavily welded in the neutral level. Four torsion-stiff lateral members and two spring bridges in the axle regions provide the transverse links. For better support of the engine, an additional unscrewable transverse link forms the front closing. The chosen material is a perlite-poor special building steel, in which no essential hardening results from welding.

Axles and Springs

The end of the gearbox shaft and the rear-axle differential are linked by a driveshaft. The rear-axle differential is essentially identical to the front-axle differential integrated into the gearbox. In the military version a driver-controlled differential lock is installed to prevent the one-sided turning of the rear wheels. With this differential lock and the fixed drive from the front and rear axles in all-wheel drive, maximum motive power with optimal steering capability is attained in off-road driving.

From the differential, half-shafts lead to the wheels. The wheel, with its 6.50 R 16 (radial) tire, is mounted on a transverse bottom triangular member to which the angled anti-sway damper is attached, and the upper transverse leaf spring is connected. The suspen-

A short time later the Iltis looked like this (top up).

Body and Top

The external form is naturally a purely utilitarian shape and is determined by the requirements for suitable ground clearance, front and rear gradients, visibility in off-road travel, and not least by the wading depth. The striking styling of the front end, including the headlights and signal lights, give it the look of a polecat (Iltis).

Through effective space utilization within the prescribed measurements, two large, sealed storage boxes could be created to the left and right of the engine compartment. On the underside of the hood a shovel can be installed and attached with a quick coupling.

The windshield can be folded down. In the normal version, weather protection is afforded by a folding top, which can be raised and lowered with a few moves. One gets in and out through four attached doors.

A variant with a plastic hardtop and two fixed doors is also available.

The body is a basinlike structure of sheet steel, made mainly of straight panels, galvanized where necessary. The body provides no carrying strength, but is screwed to the frame via elastic intermediate bearings. Painting the complete body and the frame is done simultaneously and is built up in three layers: electroplated immersion, filler, and final coat.

Testing of the Iltis began in the spring of 1976, using disguised vehicles. During the yearly summer journeys in Africa, more and more vehicles were on hand, and were thoroughly tested in extreme heat, dust, gravel, and sand. Before series production began, the Iltis in various stages of development took part in five border tests in Africa in early summer, or in Scandinavia above the Arctic Circle. Parallel to this, the Iltis was tested under extreme off-road conditions at the test center near Ingolstadt.

Beginning in October, the Bundeswehr received ten Iltis prototypes and began an exhaustive test program at Test Center 41 in Trier, as well as in several selected military units.

Parallel to this testing, the development of the prescribed sets of equipment—from radios to antitank weapons carriers—began for the military version of the Iltis, carried out by the Bundeswehr and several subcontractors. From the start it was intended that not only the vehicle, but the entire "system" with all its equipment be turned over to the Bundeswehr on schedule.

Thus, the development moved smoothly according to a fixed schedule. Preparations for production moved more and more into the foreground. In the summer of 1978 the zero series began in Ingolstadt, giving way to series production in November. The goal was to supply the Bundeswehr with production vehicles in 1978. This schedule was kept, and on November 30, 1978, the executive Army Inspector-General Reichenberger took delivery of the first 200 vehicles.

This is how the first Iltis series-production vehicles looked: Above, with top down; below, with top up.

For comparison, this page shows the Iltis test model of 1977.

A VW Iltis in military service, with a "Milan" missile.

Equipped with a camouflage net, and with all reflecting parts covered.

Here, too, everything is covered. This vehicle is already provided with the new-type camouflage.

With three-color camouflage.

With the top down, the roll bars are easy to see.

The top has not yet been camouflage-colored.

A VW Iltis of a maneuver observer/referee, marked with a white cross.

Camouflaged with tree branches.

Top photos: This is how the rear of the Iltis looks.

The engine compartment: The two radiator fans can be seen clearly, as can the left and right storage boxes.

This drawing shows all the important components.

This is how the shovel is stowed.

VW Iltis in a row; note the different color shades.

All in olive.

This vehicle was already painted bronze green

A VW Iltis of the communication troops.

e panels already have three-color camouflage.

The mount of the rotating beacon light can be seen here.

The rotating beacon can also be attached here.

Here the antenna attachment can be seen.

A Medical Corps Iltis.

The rear area can be extended.

Note the attachment of the spare wheel.

It does not get any clearer: This is obviously marked as a Medical Corps vehicle.

2. RALLY OASIS
PARIS DAKAR

STRECKENFUHRUNG - EINZELETAPPEN

1. ETAPPE PARIS - BETE - ALGIER S
2. ETAPPE ALGIER - BOU-SAADA 250 KM
3. ETAPPE BOU-SAADA - GARDATA 350 KM
4. ETAPPE GARDATA - IN SALAH 645 KM
5. ETAPPE IN SALAH REGGANE 307 KM
6. ETAPPE REGGANE - BORDI-MOKTAR - TESSALIT 800 KM
7. ETAPPE TESSALIT - GAO 520 KM
8. ETAPPE GAO - MOPTI 600 KM
9. ETAPPE MOPTI - SEGOU - KOGONI 670 KM
10. ETAPPE KOGONI - TIMBUKTU 555 KM
11. ETAPPE TIMBUKTU - GAO 424 KM
12. ETAPPE GAO - NIAMEY - QUADADOUGOU - BOBO-DIOULASSO - BAMAKO - SIGUIRI 2100 KM
13. ETAPPE SIGUIRI - LABE 665 KM
14. ETAPPE LABE - KEDOUGOU 250 KM
15. ETAPPE KEDOUGOU - TAMBACOUNDA 250 KM
16. ETAPPE TAMBACOUNDA - LINGUERE 250 KM
17. ETAPPE LINGUERE - DAKAR 250 KM

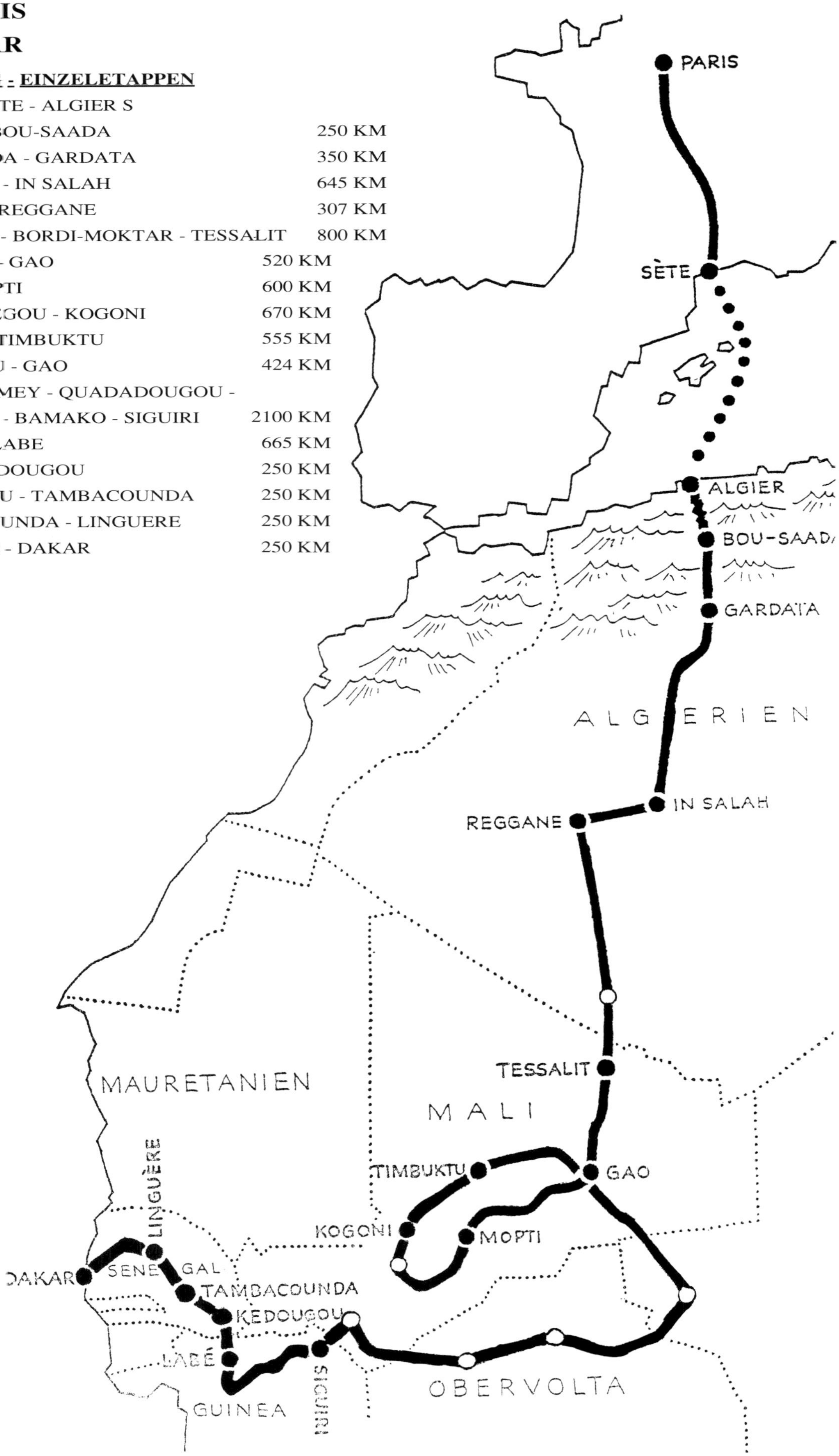

The winner of the Paris-Dakar Rally.

Historical Data

Great Success for the Volkswagen Iltis in the 2nd Paris-Dakar Oasis Rally

The VW all-wheel-drive vehicles finished first, second, fourth, and ninth.

The 2nd Paris-Dakar Oasis-Rally for motorcycles and all-terrain vehicles, held on January 1-23, 1980, turned out to be an overwhelming success for the all-wheel-drive VW Iltis entries. All four of the VW Iltis sent to Paris for this difficult off-road test reached the finish in Dakar, Senegal, after 17 stages and numerous special tests, achieving a convincing 1-2 victory. The fourth and ninth places were also taken by rally teams driving VW Iltis.

With these fine results, the all-wheel-drive Volkswagens defeated all the international competition, the off-road vehicles from Britain, France, and Japan, and proved their high degree of development and reliability impressively. The Oasis-Rally, stretching over 17 stages and some 10,000 kilometers, was a unique test of materials and, from the beginning, demanded the highest concentration, driving ability, and nervous strength of the drivers and their co-drivers. They did not have to master just a very difficult stretch through African desert regions, over washboard roads, wadis, and oases. Suddenly appearing obstacles, herds of animals, sandstorms, and other African dangers also had to be mastered to reach the finish line on the African west coast—Dakar, the capital of Senegal.

From Paris the course led first across French soil to Sete on the Mediterranean coast, then by ship to Algiers, and on the second stage to Bou Saada, and during the crossing of the Atlas Mountains, the wheat began to be separated from the chaff. At the finish of that stage, there were many breakdowns reported. On the way through central Africa, the countries of Mali, Upper Volta, Mali again, Guinea, and Senegal were covered; in numerous special stages the rally specialists could show how they and their all-wheel-drive vehicles could handle the tests they faced. The Iltis, in the hands of two German and two French teams, showed itself to be an off-road vehicle to meet the highest demands and the heaviest burdens.

Four participants at the start, four happy teams at the finish. A better finish for the Volkswagen Iltis could hardly have been wished for in this rally.

Four-wheel-drive vehicles, Class 2, Paris-Dakar Oasis-Rally:

1. Kottulinski, VW Iltis
2. Zaniroli, VW Iltis
3. Marreau, Renault 4 Sinpar
4. Ragnotti, VW Iltis
5. Neveu, Range Rover
6. Bourgoignie, Range Rover
7. Beckers, Range Rover
8. Deleforierie, Toyota
9. Gumpert, VW Iltis

10, Germonprez, Range Rover

The 2nd Oasis Rally from Paris to Dakar ended with an overwhelimng double victory for the Volkswagen Iltis. The German team of Kottulinski and Löffelmann, with racing number 137, took the first place in the four-wheel-drive category. Following them in second place was the French Iltis team of Zanirolli and Colesse. Another Iltis with the French team of Ragnotti and Vails took fourth place.

The hardtop version, a two-door civilian model.

The civilian model of the Iltis. Note the modified roll bar.

The hardtop version.

Without a peer.

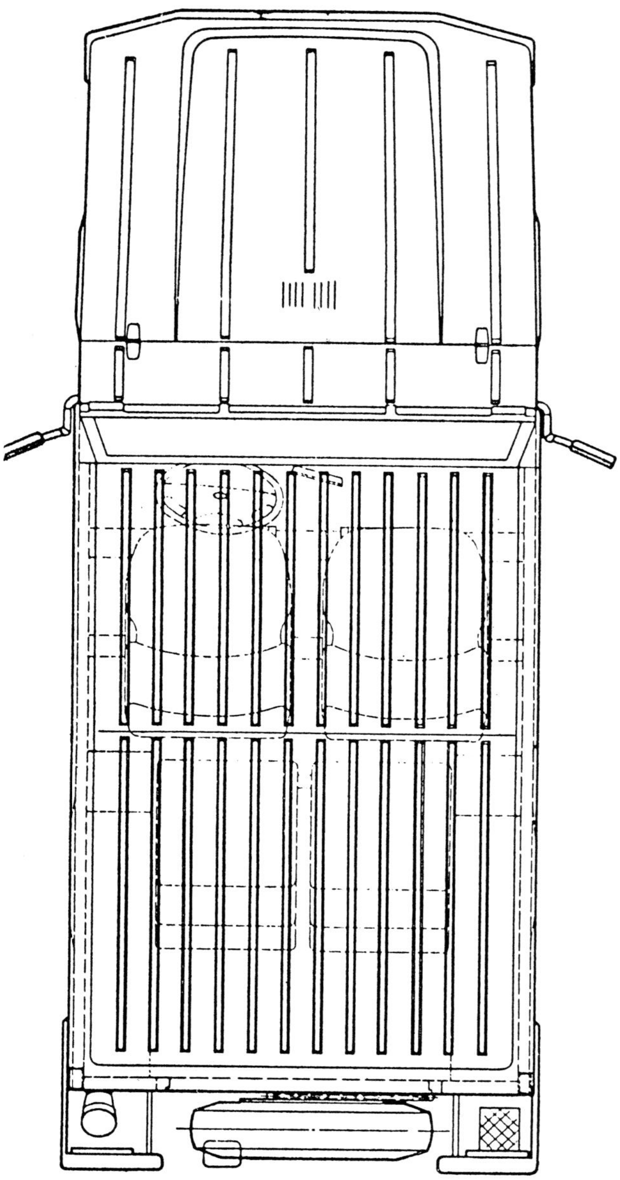

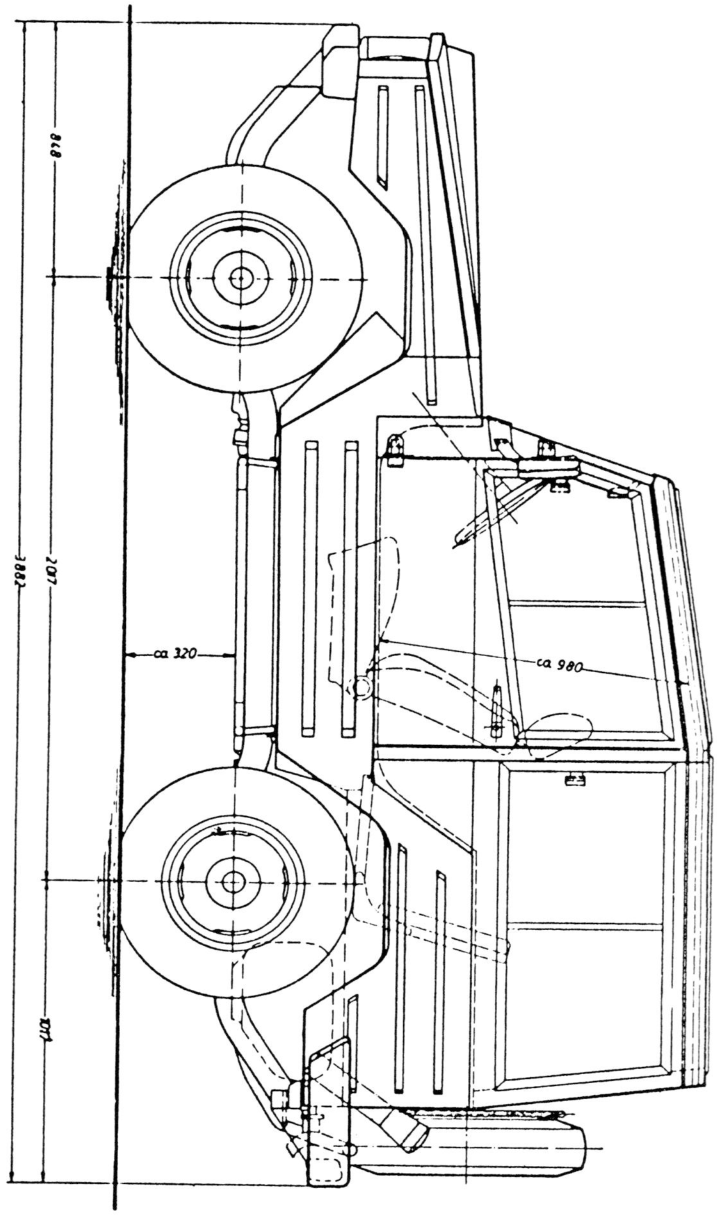

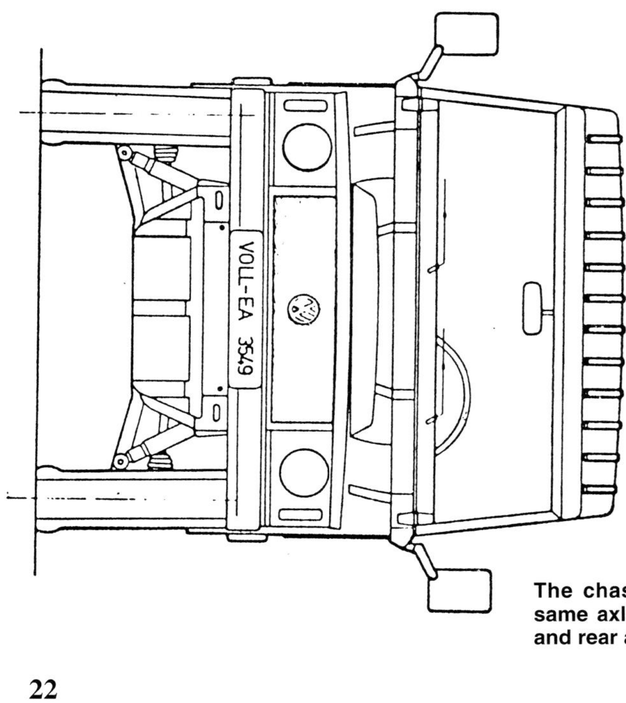

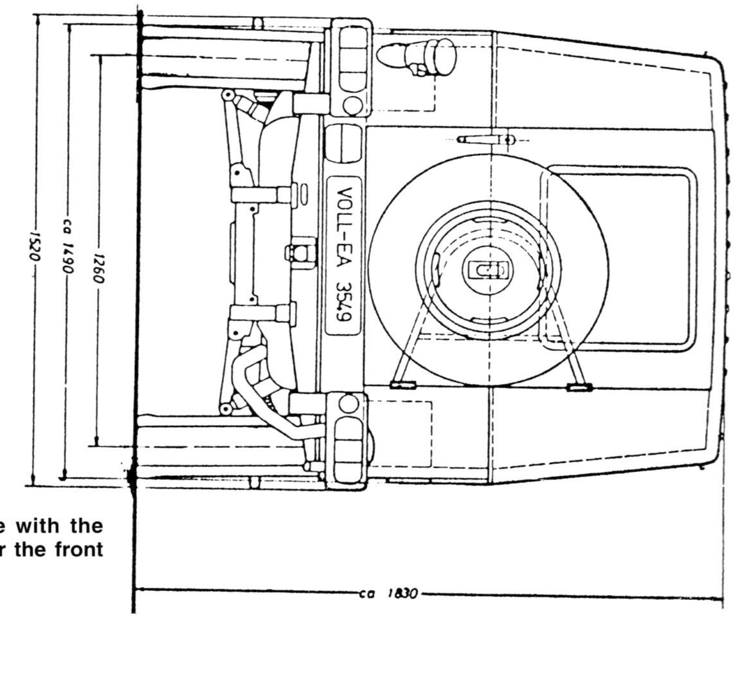

The chassis frame with the same axle parts for the front and rear axles.

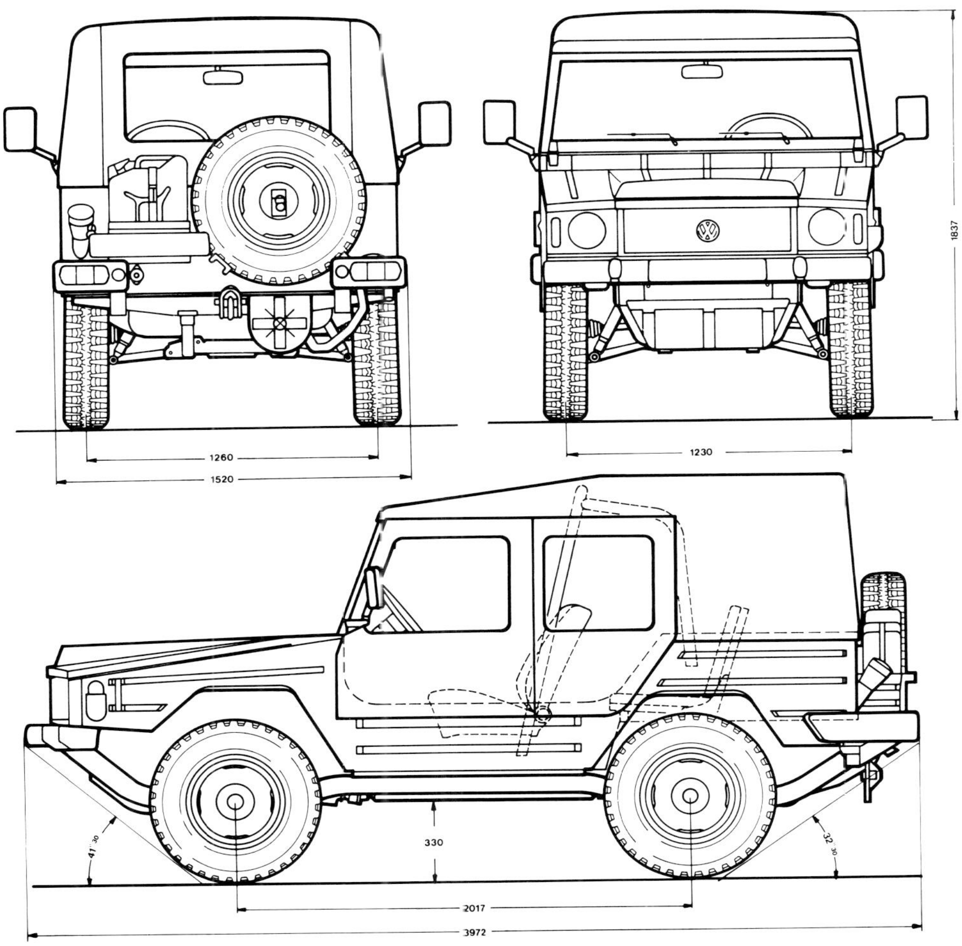

The front axle with steering.

Technical Data of the VW Iltis

Motor	
Type	Four-cylinder in-line gasoline
Bore x stroke	79.5 x 86.4 mm
Displacement	1714 cc
Compression	8.2
Fuel type	90 octane
Power	55 kW (75 HP)
at engine speed	5,000 rpm
maximum torque	135 Nm
at engine speed	2800 rpm
Carburetor	Solex 1 B1 single
Transmission	
Gear ratios 1-4	3.909, 2.277, 1.458, 1.086
Off-road gear ratio	7.603
Reverse gear ratio	7.318
Front/rear axle	5.285
Differential lock	100% front/rear (military model)
Front axle	disconnectable
Chassis and Running Gear	
Front/rear suspension	independent
Chassis frame	ladder
Tires	6.50 R 16 C 10 PR
Brakes	Two-cycle hydraulic, diagonal division, front/rear drum brakes, power brakes (military model)

Weights and Measures	
Length/width/height	3,887/1,520/1,837 mm
Wheelbase	2,017 mm
Front/rear track	1,230/1,260 mm
Turning circle	- < 11 meters
Empty weight	1,300 kg
Practical load	700 kg
Load limit	2,000 kg
Trailer limit, braked	2,000 kg
same, unbraked	685 kg
Axle load division empty	51:49%
same, fully loaded	38:62%
Performance	
Top speed	130 kph
Lowest sustained speed	4 kph
Fuel consumption, city	14.6 liters/100 km
same at 90 kph	10.5 liters/100 km
same at 120 kph	5.0 liters/100 km
Climbing Ability	
With maximum weight	to 100%
+ trailer, 685 kg	to 50%
+ trailer, 2000 kg	to 23%

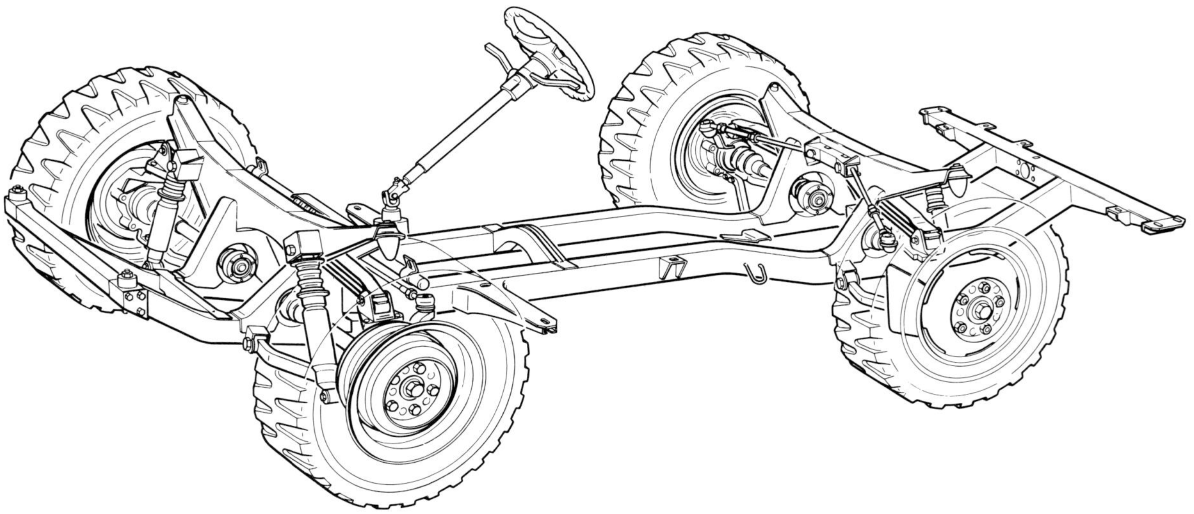

Perspective drawing of the drive train with cutaway front axle-engine block-gearbox and rear axle drive.

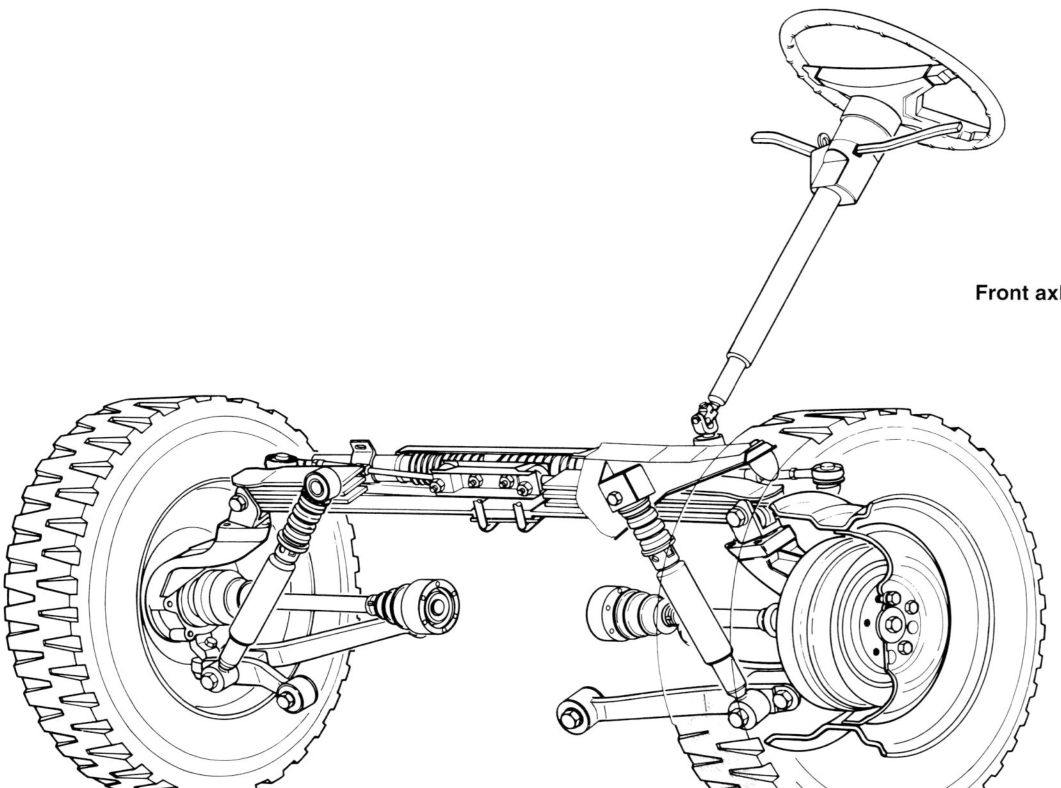

Front axle with steering.

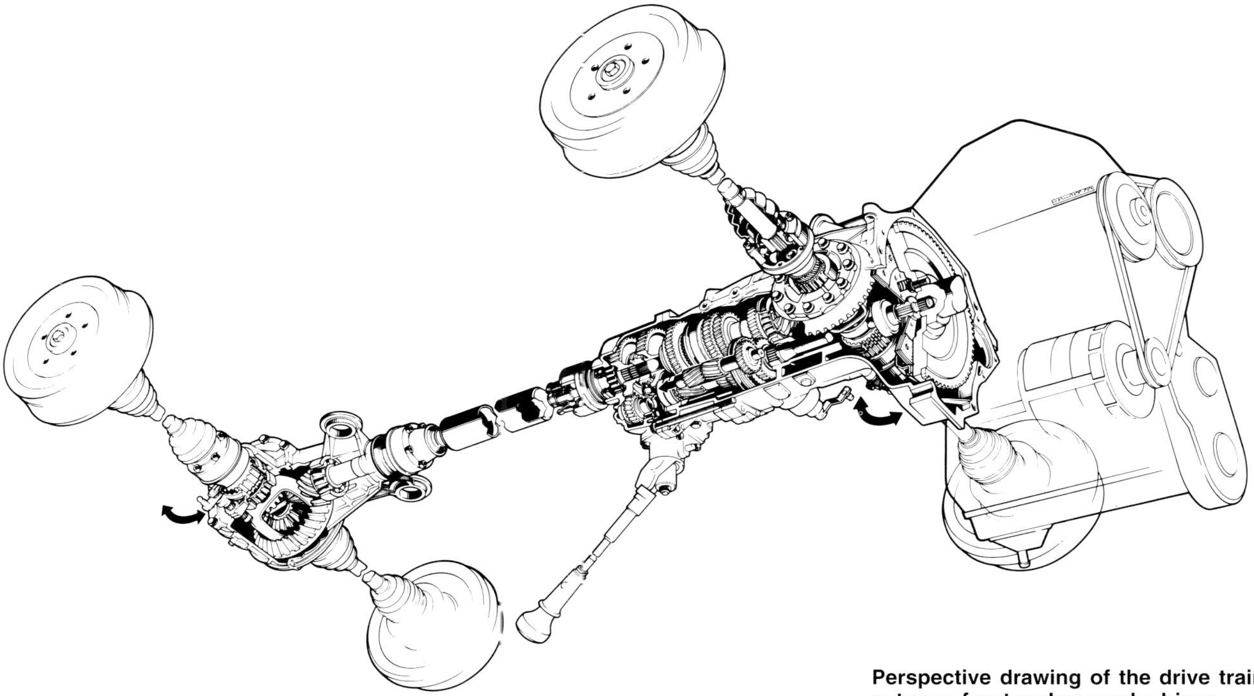

Perspective drawing of the drive train with cutaway front and rear axle drives.

Rear axle with moving parts.

The half-ton (4x4) freight-carrier "Bombardier" Model 183 YX of the Belgian Army, a VW Iltis built under license.

The Model 183 YK Bombardier built under license for the Belgian Army, with single-axle trailer.

The medical version of the Model 183 YX Bombardier, in service with a Belgian infantry battalion.

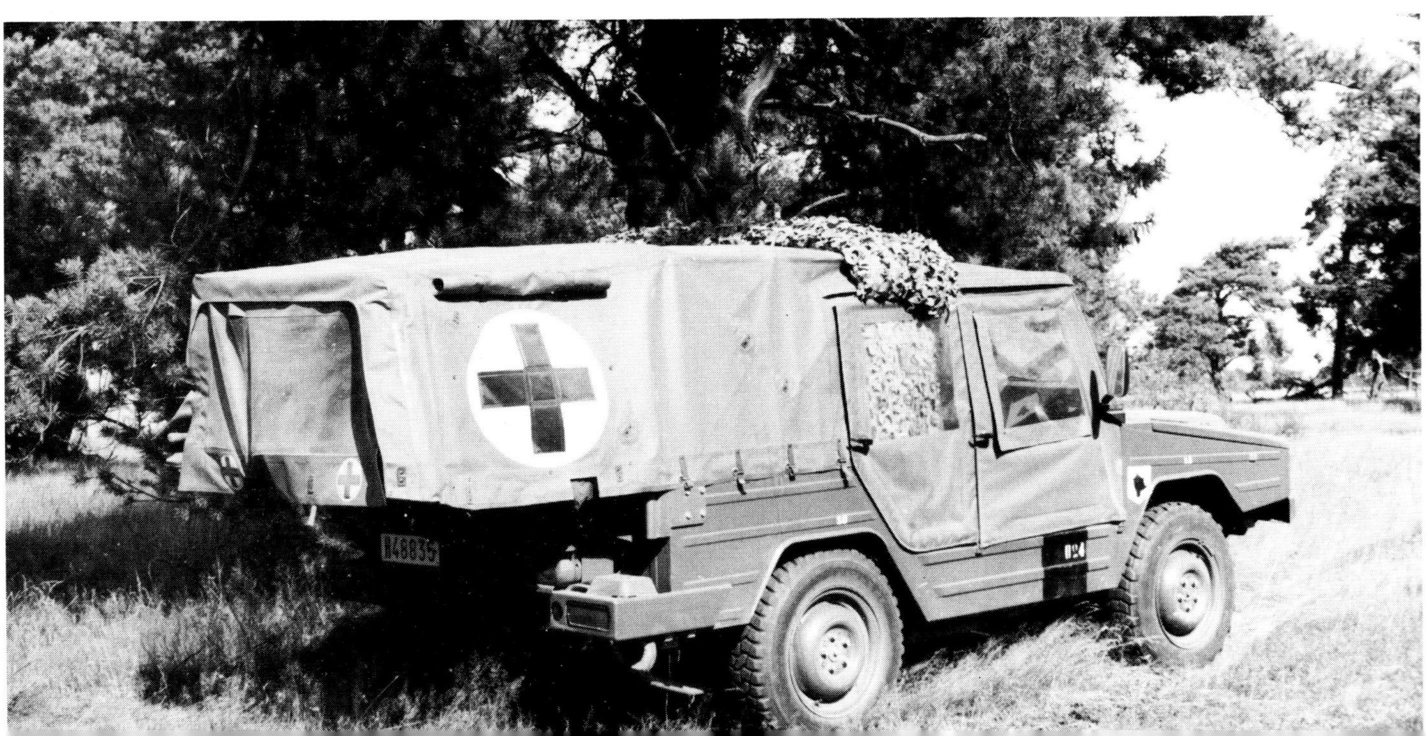